Copyright © 2023 by Cameron Bailey (Author)

All rights reserved. No part of this book may be reproduced or utilized in any form or by any means, electronic or mechanical, including photocopying, recording or by any information storage and retrieval system, without permission in writing from the publisher, except for brief quotations in critical articles or reviews.

The content of this book is based on various sources and is intended for educational and entertainment purposes only. While the author has made every effort to ensure the accuracy, completeness, and reliability of the information provided, the information may be subject to errors, omissions, or inaccuracies. Therefore, the author makes no warranties, express or implied, regarding the content of this book.

Readers are advised to seek the guidance of a licensed professional before attempting any techniques or actions outlined in this book. The author is not responsible for any losses, damages, or injuries that may arise from the use of information contained within. The information provided in this book is not intended to be a substitute for professional advice, and readers should not rely solely on the information presented.

By reading this book, readers acknowledge that the author is not providing legal, financial, medical, or professional advice. Any reliance on the information contained in this book is solely at the reader's own risk.

Thank you for selecting this book as a valuable source of knowledge and inspiration. Our aim is to provide you with insights and information that will enrich your understanding and enhance your personal growth. We appreciate your decision to embark on this journey of discovery with us, and we hope that this book will exceed your expectations and leave a lasting impact on your life.

Title: Overcoming Self-Doubt
Subtitle: Identifying and Conquering the Barriers to Confidence

Series: The Secrets of Self-Confidence: A Comprehensive Guide to Achieving Your Goals
Author: Cameron Bailey

Table of Contents

Introduction 5
Overcoming Self-Doubt: Identifying and Conquering the Barriers to Confidence 5
What are self-confidence blocks? 8
How to identify your self-confidence blocks 13

Chapter 1: The different types of self-confidence blocks 15
External blocks 15
Internal blocks 18

Chapter 2: How to identify your self-confidence blocks 21
Take a self-assessment 21
Talk to a therapist or counselor 24
Pay attention to your thoughts and feelings 27

Chapter 3: Overcoming your self-confidence blocks 30
Challenge your negative thoughts 30
Focus on your strengths 33
Set realistic goals 35
Take risks 38
Surround yourself with positive people 41
Practice positive self-talk 44

Chapter 4: Maintaining your self-confidence 47

Continue to challenge yourself 47
Be patient 50
Celebrate your successes 53

Chapter 5: Dealing with setbacks **55**
Don't give up 55
Learn from your mistakes 58
Don't compare yourself to others 61
Celebrate your successes 64

Chapter 6: Finding your inner confidence **68**
What is inner confidence? 68
How to find your inner confidence 71

Conclusion **76**
The importance of inner confidence 76
How to continue to build your inner confidence 78

Wordbook **81**
Supplementary Materials **83**

Introduction
Overcoming Self-Doubt: Identifying and Conquering the Barriers to Confidence

Self-confidence is a critical trait that allows us to tackle challenges, achieve our goals, and pursue our dreams. However, for many people, self-doubt and negative self-talk can get in the way of feeling confident and reaching their full potential. In this book, we will explore the topic of overcoming self-doubt and identifying and conquering the barriers to confidence.

Chapter 1: The Different Types of Self-Confidence Blocks

To begin, we will examine the various types of self-confidence blocks that people commonly experience. These include external blocks, such as societal pressures or negative feedback from others, and internal blocks, such as negative self-talk or limiting beliefs about oneself. By understanding the different types of blocks, readers will be better equipped to identify which ones they are experiencing and how to address them.

Chapter 2: How to Identify Your Self-Confidence Blocks

In this chapter, we will explore different methods for identifying self-confidence blocks. These methods may include taking a self-assessment, talking to a therapist or counselor, or simply paying attention to one's thoughts and feelings. By learning to identify these blocks, readers will be better equipped to take action to overcome them.

Chapter 3: Overcoming Your Self-Confidence Blocks

This chapter will provide practical strategies for overcoming self-confidence blocks. Strategies may include challenging negative thoughts, focusing on one's strengths, setting realistic goals, taking risks, surrounding oneself with positive people, and practicing positive self-talk. By taking action to overcome self-confidence blocks, readers will be able to feel more confident and pursue their goals with greater ease.

Chapter 4: Maintaining Your Self-Confidence

In this chapter, we will explore strategies for maintaining self-confidence over time. These may include continuing to challenge oneself, being patient with oneself, and celebrating successes. By focusing on maintaining self-confidence over time, readers will be better equipped to overcome setbacks and continue to make progress towards their goals.

Chapter 5: Dealing with Setbacks

Setbacks are an inevitable part of life, and in this chapter, we will explore strategies for bouncing back from setbacks and continuing to build self-confidence. These strategies may include not giving up, learning from mistakes, not comparing oneself to others, and celebrating successes. By learning to cope with setbacks in a healthy way, readers will be able to maintain their self-confidence even in the face of adversity.

Chapter 6: Finding Your Inner Confidence

In this chapter, we will explore the concept of inner confidence, which is a deeper and more enduring type of confidence that comes from within. We will discuss what inner confidence is, how to find it, and how to cultivate it over time. By developing inner confidence, readers will be better equipped to overcome self-doubt and achieve their goals with greater ease and clarity.

Conclusion:

In the conclusion, we will tie together all the themes explored in the book and emphasize the importance of building inner confidence as a way to overcome self-doubt and achieve one's goals. We will also provide readers with practical tips and strategies for continuing to build their self-confidence over time. By providing readers with the tools they need to conquer their self-confidence blocks, this book will help them to feel more confident, capable, and empowered in their lives.

What are self-confidence blocks?

Self-confidence is a critical trait that can help us achieve our goals, develop positive relationships, and live a fulfilling life. However, for many people, self-confidence can be hindered by self-doubt and negative self-talk. In this chapter, we will explore the concept of self-confidence blocks, what they are, and how they can hinder our self-confidence.

What are Self-Confidence Blocks?

Self-confidence blocks are internal or external barriers that can prevent us from feeling confident and pursuing our goals. These blocks can come in many different forms and may stem from a variety of sources. Some common examples of self-confidence blocks include:

1. Negative self-talk: Negative self-talk refers to the inner voice that criticizes us, puts us down, and undermines our self-esteem. When we engage in negative self-talk, we may focus on our flaws, mistakes, and shortcomings, which can prevent us from feeling confident and capable.

2. Limiting beliefs: Limiting beliefs are deeply held beliefs about ourselves that may not be accurate or true. These beliefs can be formed by past experiences, cultural or societal norms, or negative feedback from others. When we hold onto limiting beliefs, we may see ourselves as incapable,

unworthy, or undeserving of success, which can hinder our self-confidence.

3. Fear of failure: Fear of failure is a common self-confidence block that can prevent us from taking risks or pursuing our goals. When we fear failure, we may avoid trying new things, taking on challenges, or pursuing our passions, which can prevent us from developing our skills and feeling confident in our abilities.

4. Comparison to others: When we compare ourselves to others, we may feel inadequate or inferior, which can undermine our self-confidence. We may focus on others' strengths, successes, and achievements, and compare them to our own, leading us to feel less capable or worthy.

5. Negative feedback from others: Negative feedback from others, whether it is constructive criticism or outright criticism, can be a self-confidence block. When we receive negative feedback, we may internalize it and believe that we are not capable or talented, which can undermine our self-confidence.

Conclusion:

Self-confidence blocks are common barriers that can prevent us from feeling confident, pursuing our goals, and living a fulfilling life. By understanding the different types of self-confidence blocks and how they can hinder our self-confidence, we can begin to identify and address them. In the next chapter, we will explore different methods for identifying self-confidence blocks and taking action to overcome them.

Why are self-confidence blocks important to identify?

Self-confidence is a crucial trait that can have a significant impact on our personal and professional lives. When we feel confident, we are more likely to pursue our goals, take risks, and engage in meaningful relationships. However, self-confidence blocks can prevent us from feeling confident and achieving our full potential. In this chapter, we will explore why identifying self-confidence blocks is essential and the consequences of not addressing them.

Why are self-confidence blocks important to identify?

1. Preventing self-sabotage: When we have self-confidence blocks, we may engage in self-sabotaging behaviors that can prevent us from achieving our goals. For example, if we have a fear of failure, we may avoid taking risks or pursuing our passions, which can prevent us from developing our skills and achieving our dreams.

2. Improving our relationships: Self-confidence blocks can also impact our relationships with others. When we lack confidence, we may struggle to communicate effectively,

express ourselves, or connect with others. This can lead to difficulties in our personal and professional relationships, ultimately hindering our success and happiness.

3. Enhancing our performance: Self-confidence is essential for achieving success in our personal and professional lives. When we lack confidence, we may not perform as well as we are capable of, which can limit our potential and opportunities. By identifying and addressing our self-confidence blocks, we can enhance our performance and achieve greater success.

4. Increasing our self-awareness: Identifying our self-confidence blocks can help us become more self-aware and understand ourselves better. By recognizing the patterns, beliefs, and behaviors that are holding us back, we can take steps to address them and develop a deeper understanding of ourselves and our potential.

5. Boosting our self-esteem: Finally, identifying and overcoming self-confidence blocks can boost our self-esteem and improve our overall well-being. When we feel confident, we are more likely to have a positive self-image, take care of ourselves, and pursue our goals with enthusiasm and determination.

Conclusion:

Self-confidence blocks can prevent us from achieving our full potential and living a fulfilling life. By identifying these blocks and taking steps to address them, we can prevent self-sabotage, improve our relationships, enhance our performance, increase our self-awareness, and boost our self-esteem. In the next chapter, we will explore different methods for identifying self-confidence blocks and taking action to overcome them.

How to identify your self-confidence blocks

Identifying our self-confidence blocks is the first step in overcoming them and developing greater confidence. In this chapter, we will explore several effective methods for identifying self-confidence blocks, including taking a self-assessment, talking to a therapist or counselor, and paying attention to our thoughts and feelings. By becoming aware of our self-confidence blocks, we can begin to take steps to overcome them and develop greater confidence.

How to identify your self-confidence blocks:

1. Take a self-assessment: Self-assessments can be a helpful tool for identifying our self-confidence blocks. There are many online assessments available that can help us identify our strengths, weaknesses, and areas of self-doubt. These assessments can provide insight into the patterns, beliefs, and behaviors that are holding us back from feeling confident and achieving our goals.

2. Talk to a therapist or counselor: Another effective way to identify our self-confidence blocks is to talk to a therapist or counselor. A trained mental health professional can help us explore our thoughts, feelings, and behaviors and identify any patterns or beliefs that may be contributing to our lack of confidence. Therapy can also provide us with

tools and strategies for overcoming our self-confidence blocks and developing greater confidence.

3. Pay attention to our thoughts and feelings: Finally, paying attention to our thoughts and feelings can be an effective way to identify our self-confidence blocks. When we experience feelings of self-doubt or insecurity, it can be helpful to ask ourselves what thoughts or beliefs are contributing to these feelings. By becoming more aware of our negative self-talk and limiting beliefs, we can begin to challenge them and develop a more positive and confident mindset.

Conclusion:

Identifying our self-confidence blocks is essential for developing greater confidence and achieving our goals. By taking a self-assessment, talking to a therapist or counselor, and paying attention to our thoughts and feelings, we can become more aware of the patterns, beliefs, and behaviors that are holding us back. With this awareness, we can begin to take steps to overcome our self-confidence blocks and develop greater confidence and self-esteem. In the next chapter, we will explore effective strategies for overcoming self-confidence blocks and developing greater confidence.

Chapter 1: The different types of self-confidence blocks

External blocks

Self-confidence blocks can arise from a variety of sources, including internal beliefs and external factors. In this chapter, we will explore the different types of self-confidence blocks, including external blocks and internal blocks.

External blocks are factors outside of ourselves that can impact our confidence levels. These factors can come from our environment, other people, or societal pressures. Here are some common external blocks that can impact our self-confidence:

1. Criticism and judgment from others: When we receive criticism or negative feedback from others, it can impact our confidence levels. This can be especially true if the criticism comes from someone we respect or admire. We may begin to doubt ourselves and our abilities, leading to a decrease in self-confidence.

2. Social comparison: Comparing ourselves to others can be a significant source of self-doubt and insecurity. When we see others succeeding or appearing to have their lives together, we may feel inadequate or like we are falling behind. Social media can exacerbate this problem by giving

us a constant stream of perfectly curated lives to compare ourselves to.

3. Rejection or failure: Experiencing rejection or failure can be a significant blow to our self-confidence. Whether it's a job rejection, a failed relationship, or a project that didn't go as planned, these setbacks can lead us to doubt our abilities and worth.

4. Lack of support: When we lack support from those around us, it can impact our self-confidence. Whether it's feeling like we don't have a strong support system or feeling like we don't have anyone to turn to in times of need, the absence of support can leave us feeling alone and insecure.

5. Societal pressures: Societal pressures, such as beauty standards or expectations around career success, can impact our self-confidence. When we feel like we don't measure up to these standards, we may begin to doubt ourselves and our abilities.

So, how can we overcome these external blocks and develop greater self-confidence? Here are some strategies:

1. Develop a support system: Surrounding ourselves with people who believe in us and support us can be a significant source of confidence. Seek out friends, family members, or mentors who you can turn to for encouragement and advice.

2. Limit exposure to negativity: While it's impossible to completely avoid criticism or negative feedback, we can limit our exposure to it. This may mean unfollowing social media accounts that make you feel bad about yourself or setting boundaries with people who are overly critical.

3. Challenge negative beliefs: When we experience external blocks, we may develop negative beliefs about ourselves and our abilities. Challenging these beliefs and reframing them in a more positive light can help us develop greater confidence.

4. Set realistic goals: Setting achievable goals and working towards them can help us build confidence in our abilities. When we accomplish something, no matter how small, it can help us feel more capable and confident.

5. Practice self-care: Taking care of ourselves physically, mentally, and emotionally can help us feel more confident and resilient. This may include activities like exercise, meditation, or therapy.

In conclusion, external blocks can have a significant impact on our self-confidence. By understanding these blocks and developing strategies to overcome them, we can develop greater confidence and resilience in the face of external challenges. In the next section, we will explore internal blocks and how they impact our self-confidence.

Internal blocks

Internal blocks are the mental and emotional obstacles that prevent us from feeling self-confident. Unlike external blocks, which are often more tangible and easier to identify, internal blocks can be subtle and deeply ingrained in our beliefs and thought patterns.

There are many different types of internal blocks that can hinder our self-confidence. Some common examples include:

1. Negative self-talk: Negative self-talk is the inner voice that tells us we're not good enough, smart enough, or capable enough to succeed. This type of internal block can be especially damaging, as it can lead to a self-fulfilling prophecy where we believe we can't succeed, so we don't even try.

2. Perfectionism: Perfectionism is the belief that we need to be perfect in order to be successful. This type of internal block can be paralyzing, as it can prevent us from taking action or trying new things for fear of making mistakes.

3. Fear of failure: Fear of failure is a common internal block that can hold us back from reaching our full potential. When we're afraid of failing, we may avoid taking risks or

trying new things, which can prevent us from achieving our goals.

4. Low self-esteem: Low self-esteem is the belief that we're not worthy or deserving of success. This type of internal block can be especially damaging, as it can lead to a cycle of negative self-talk and self-sabotage.

5. Past traumas or negative experiences: Past traumas or negative experiences can create internal blocks by shaping our beliefs and thought patterns. For example, if we've experienced rejection or criticism in the past, we may develop a fear of being judged or a belief that we're not good enough.

Identifying internal blocks can be challenging, as they often operate beneath the surface of our conscious awareness. However, there are some strategies that can help us uncover these blocks and start to overcome them:

1. Practice mindfulness: Mindfulness involves paying attention to our thoughts and feelings without judgment. By practicing mindfulness, we can start to become more aware of our internal dialogue and identify patterns of negative self-talk or self-sabotage.

2. Keep a journal: Keeping a journal can be a helpful tool for identifying internal blocks. By writing down our

thoughts and feelings, we can start to see patterns and identify areas where we may be holding ourselves back.

3. Seek feedback: Asking for feedback from trusted friends, family members, or colleagues can be a helpful way to identify internal blocks. Others may be able to see patterns or behaviors that we're not aware of, and provide valuable insights into areas where we may be holding ourselves back.

4. Work with a therapist or coach: Working with a therapist or coach can be an effective way to identify and overcome internal blocks. A trained professional can provide guidance and support as we work to identify and overcome limiting beliefs and patterns of negative self-talk.

By identifying and overcoming internal blocks, we can start to build our self-confidence and achieve our goals. While it can be challenging to uncover these blocks, the rewards of increased self-confidence and self-awareness are well worth the effort.

Chapter 2: How to identify your self-confidence blocks

Take a self-assessment

Taking a self-assessment is an effective way to identify your self-confidence blocks. Self-assessments are a valuable tool for gaining insight into your thoughts, feelings, and behaviors. Here are some steps to help you take a self-assessment to identify your self-confidence blocks:

1. Identify areas of your life where you lack confidence: Begin by identifying areas of your life where you lack confidence. This could be in your personal life, work life, social life, or any other area where you feel unsure of yourself.

2. Look for patterns: Look for patterns in your behavior and thoughts. Do you always doubt your abilities in a particular area? Do you tend to avoid certain situations or tasks because you lack confidence? Identifying patterns can help you identify the root cause of your self-confidence block.

3. Reflect on past experiences: Reflect on past experiences where you felt confident and successful, as well as those where you felt self-doubt. What were the differences between these experiences? What factors contributed to your success or lack of confidence? Identifying these factors can help you recognize what triggers your self-confidence blocks.

4. Use self-reflection tools: There are many self-reflection tools available, such as journaling or mindfulness exercises, that can help you gain insight into your thoughts and feelings. Use these tools to reflect on your self-confidence blocks and identify any underlying issues.

5. Seek feedback: Ask friends, family members, or coworkers for feedback on your strengths and areas for improvement. This feedback can help you gain a better understanding of how others perceive you and where you may be lacking confidence.

6. Use self-assessment tools: There are many self-assessment tools available that can help you identify your self-confidence blocks. Some of these tools include personality tests, emotional intelligence assessments, and self-confidence quizzes. These tools can provide you with a more objective view of your strengths and weaknesses.

Remember, taking a self-assessment is just the first step in identifying your self-confidence blocks. It's important to also seek out the help of a therapist or counselor if you're struggling to identify the root cause of your self-confidence issues. With time, effort, and the right tools, you can learn to overcome your self-confidence blocks and become more self-assured and confident in all areas of your life.

Talk to a therapist or counselor

Talking to a therapist or counselor can be an effective way to identify and address self-confidence blocks. These professionals are trained to help individuals identify the root causes of their self-doubt and develop strategies for overcoming it. Here are some ways in which talking to a therapist or counselor can be beneficial:

1. Provide a Safe Space to Explore Your Feelings One of the primary benefits of talking to a therapist or counselor is that they provide a safe and non-judgmental space for you to explore your feelings. They will listen actively to what you have to say and offer support and guidance throughout the process. This can be especially helpful if you find it difficult to open up to friends or family members about your self-doubt.

2. Help You Identify Your Triggers Therapists and counselors can also help you identify your triggers or the specific situations or people that tend to trigger your self-doubt. They will help you to understand why these triggers have such an impact on you and work with you to develop coping strategies to manage them better.

3. Teach You Coping Strategies Therapists and counselors can teach you various coping strategies to help you manage your self-doubt. These may include mindfulness

techniques, visualization, cognitive-behavioral therapy, or other evidence-based approaches that have been shown to be effective in improving self-confidence.

4. Provide Feedback and Support A therapist or counselor can offer objective feedback on your progress and provide ongoing support as you work towards overcoming your self-confidence blocks. They can help you stay motivated, focused, and on track towards achieving your goals.

5. Improve Your Communication Skills Talking to a therapist or counselor can also help you improve your communication skills, which can be useful in a variety of contexts, including personal and professional relationships. They can teach you how to express your needs and wants more effectively and communicate more assertively.

6. Improve Your Overall Mental Health Lastly, talking to a therapist or counselor can help improve your overall mental health. Self-doubt and low self-esteem can lead to a range of mental health issues, such as anxiety and depression. By addressing these issues early on, you can reduce your risk of developing more severe mental health problems in the future.

In conclusion, talking to a therapist or counselor can be a valuable tool in identifying and overcoming self-confidence blocks. These professionals can help you understand the root causes of your self-doubt, teach you coping strategies, and provide ongoing support to help you build your self-confidence over time.

Pay attention to your thoughts and feelings

Another effective way to identify your self-confidence blocks is to pay attention to your thoughts and feelings. This is an introspective process that requires you to be honest with yourself about how you feel and what you think about yourself and your abilities. Here are some steps to help you in this process:

1. Keep a journal

One way to become more aware of your thoughts and feelings is to keep a journal. Writing down your thoughts and feelings in a journal can help you identify patterns in your thinking and behavior. This can help you see the areas where you need to work on building your self-confidence.

2. Notice negative self-talk

Negative self-talk can be a significant self-confidence block. Negative self-talk is when you tell yourself things like, "I'm not good enough," "I'm not smart enough," or "I'm not attractive enough." These negative thoughts can become ingrained and affect your self-esteem. Start paying attention to your thoughts and notice when you're engaging in negative self-talk.

3. Identify your triggers

Certain situations or people may trigger negative thoughts and feelings. These triggers can be a self-confidence block. Identify what triggers negative thoughts and feelings for you. Once you're aware of these triggers, you can work on developing strategies to cope with them.

4. Monitor your emotions

Your emotions can be a clue to your self-confidence blocks. If you feel anxious or fearful in certain situations, it may be because you lack confidence in that area. Take note of your emotions and try to identify the root cause of them. Once you understand the source of your emotions, you can work on addressing the underlying issues.

5. Seek feedback

Getting feedback from others can be a helpful way to identify your self-confidence blocks. Ask friends, family members, or colleagues for their honest feedback on your strengths and weaknesses. This can help you see areas where you need to work on building your self-confidence.

6. Practice mindfulness

Practicing mindfulness can help you become more aware of your thoughts and feelings. Mindfulness is a technique that involves paying attention to the present moment without judgment. This can help you become more aware of negative thoughts and feelings and learn to let them go.

In conclusion, paying attention to your thoughts and feelings can help you identify your self-confidence blocks. It's important to be honest with yourself about your strengths and weaknesses so you can work on building your self-confidence in the areas where you need it most.

Chapter 3: Overcoming your self-confidence blocks
Challenge your negative thoughts

Negative thoughts can be a major obstacle to building self-confidence. They can hold us back, make us feel unworthy, and prevent us from pursuing our goals and dreams. But the good news is that negative thoughts can be challenged and overcome. In this chapter, we will explore how to identify and challenge negative thoughts, and provide strategies to help you overcome self-doubt.

Identifying Negative Thoughts

The first step to overcoming negative thoughts is to become aware of them. Negative thoughts can take many different forms, but some common examples include:

- All-or-nothing thinking: Seeing things in black-and-white terms, without considering any shades of grey.

- Overgeneralization: Drawing sweeping conclusions based on a single negative experience.

- Catastrophizing: Assuming the worst possible outcome in a given situation.

- Personalization: Assuming that negative events are a direct result of your own actions or characteristics.

- Mind reading: Assuming that you know what others are thinking, and that they are judging you negatively.

If you find yourself engaging in any of these types of thinking, it's important to challenge these thoughts and replace them with more positive, realistic ones.

Challenging Negative Thoughts

Once you've identified your negative thoughts, you can start to challenge them. Here are some strategies that may help:

1. Question the evidence: Ask yourself whether there is any concrete evidence to support your negative thought. Often, our negative thoughts are based on assumptions or irrational beliefs, rather than facts.

2. Consider alternative explanations: Try to come up with alternative explanations for the situation at hand. Is there a different way to interpret what happened that is more positive or realistic?

3. Put it in perspective: Ask yourself whether the situation is really as catastrophic as you're making it out to be. Is it possible that you're blowing things out of proportion?

4. Focus on the positive: Make a conscious effort to focus on the positive aspects of the situation. What are the things that went well, or that you can learn from?

5. Use positive affirmations: Repeat positive affirmations to yourself, such as "I am capable," "I am

worthy," or "I am enough." These can help to counteract negative self-talk and build self-confidence.

6. Seek support: Reach out to friends, family, or a therapist for support and encouragement. Talking through your negative thoughts with someone else can help you gain perspective and develop more positive ways of thinking.

Overcoming self-doubt takes time and effort, but it is possible. By challenging your negative thoughts and replacing them with more positive, realistic ones, you can build your self-confidence and achieve your goals. Remember, you are capable and worthy, and you have the power to overcome self-doubt and achieve success.

Focus on your strengths

Focusing on your strengths is an essential aspect of overcoming self-confidence blocks. When you focus on your strengths, you can build your confidence and start to see yourself in a more positive light. Here are some strategies for focusing on your strengths:

1. Identify your strengths: Take some time to think about your skills, talents, and achievements. What are you good at? What have you accomplished in the past? Make a list of your strengths and refer to it often to remind yourself of what you're capable of.

2. Use your strengths: Once you've identified your strengths, find ways to use them in your daily life. If you're good at writing, start a blog or write a journal. If you're good at public speaking, look for opportunities to speak in public or join a Toastmasters group. When you use your strengths, you'll feel more confident and fulfilled.

3. Surround yourself with positive people: Spend time with people who support and encourage you. They can help you identify your strengths and provide the support you need to develop them further.

4. Develop new strengths: While it's important to focus on your existing strengths, it's also important to develop new ones. Learning new skills or taking on new

challenges can help you build your confidence and see yourself in a more positive light.

5. Acknowledge your achievements: When you accomplish something, no matter how small, take the time to acknowledge it. Celebrate your achievements and use them as motivation to continue growing and developing your strengths.

6. Practice self-compassion: Remember that everyone has strengths and weaknesses, and it's okay to make mistakes. Practice self-compassion and be kind to yourself, even when things don't go as planned.

By focusing on your strengths, you can start to overcome your self-confidence blocks and develop a more positive self-image. Remember to be patient with yourself and celebrate your progress along the way.

Set realistic goals

Setting realistic goals is an important aspect of overcoming self-confidence blocks. When we set goals that are too high or unrealistic, we set ourselves up for failure, which can lead to a further decrease in confidence. In this section, we will discuss how to set realistic goals that can help you overcome your self-confidence blocks.

1. Identify your values and priorities

Before setting goals, it's important to identify your values and priorities. What is important to you? What do you want to achieve in your life? Understanding your values and priorities can help you set goals that are aligned with what truly matters to you.

2. Be specific

When setting goals, it's important to be specific. Vague goals such as "be more confident" or "be happier" are difficult to achieve because they are not specific enough. Instead, set specific goals such as "speak up in meetings" or "take a yoga class twice a week."

3. Make your goals measurable

Making your goals measurable means that you can track your progress and know when you have achieved your goal. For example, if your goal is to speak up in meetings, you could measure your progress by the number of times you speak up in a meeting.

4. Break your goals down into smaller steps

Breaking your goals down into smaller steps can make them feel more achievable. For example, if your goal is to take a yoga class twice a week, you could break it down into smaller steps such as finding a yoga studio, signing up for a class, and attending the first class.

5. Be realistic

When setting goals, it's important to be realistic. Setting goals that are too difficult or unrealistic can lead to disappointment and a decrease in confidence. Be honest with yourself about what you can realistically achieve given your current circumstances.

6. Focus on the process, not just the outcome

While it's important to have a specific goal in mind, it's also important to focus on the process of achieving that goal. This means focusing on the small steps you need to take to get there, rather than just the end result. Celebrate small victories along the way and don't be too hard on yourself if you experience setbacks.

7. Stay motivated

Staying motivated can be challenging, especially if you encounter setbacks or obstacles along the way. One way to stay motivated is to remind yourself of why you set the goal in the first place. Visualize yourself achieving your goal and how it will make you feel. Additionally, find support from others who can encourage and motivate you along the way.

In conclusion, setting realistic goals is an important step in overcoming self-confidence blocks. By identifying your values and priorities, being specific, making your goals measurable, breaking them down into smaller steps, being realistic, focusing on the process, and staying motivated, you can achieve your goals and build your confidence.

Take risks

Taking risks is an essential aspect of overcoming self-confidence blocks. When we allow ourselves to step out of our comfort zones and take calculated risks, we become more confident in our abilities and increase our chances of success. However, taking risks can be scary, especially if we have experienced failures or setbacks in the past. In this section, we will discuss how taking risks can help you overcome self-doubt and how to do it in a way that feels comfortable and safe for you.

The Benefits of Taking Risks When we take risks, we expose ourselves to new experiences and opportunities. This can lead to personal and professional growth, and help us overcome our self-confidence blocks. Here are some of the benefits of taking risks:

1. Builds Confidence: When we take risks and succeed, it boosts our confidence and self-esteem. This can lead to a positive cycle where we continue to take risks and achieve success.

2. Expands Comfort Zones: Taking risks requires us to step outside of our comfort zones. As we become more comfortable with taking risks, our comfort zones expand, allowing us to take on even greater challenges.

3. Increases Resilience: Taking risks involves the possibility of failure or setbacks. By learning to bounce back from these failures, we become more resilient and better equipped to handle future challenges.

4. Creates Opportunities: Taking risks can lead to new opportunities and experiences that we may not have encountered otherwise. This can lead to personal and professional growth and fulfillment.

How to Take Risks While taking risks can be beneficial, it is essential to approach them in a way that feels comfortable and safe for you. Here are some tips on how to take risks effectively:

1. Identify Your Goals: Before taking any risks, it is essential to identify your goals and what you hope to achieve. This will help you determine which risks are worth taking and which are not.

2. Start Small: Taking small risks can help you build up your confidence and comfort level. Start with something small, such as trying a new restaurant or taking a different route to work.

3. Weigh the Pros and Cons: Before taking any risks, it is essential to weigh the potential risks and benefits. This will help you make an informed decision about whether or not to proceed.

4. Be Prepared: Taking risks involves the possibility of failure or setbacks. Be prepared for the worst-case scenario and have a plan in place to deal with any potential issues.

5. Learn From Failure: Not all risks will pay off, and that's okay. Use any failures or setbacks as an opportunity to learn and grow.

6. Celebrate Your Successes: When you do take a risk and succeed, take the time to celebrate your successes. This will help you build confidence and momentum for future risks.

In conclusion, taking risks is an essential aspect of overcoming self-confidence blocks. By building confidence, expanding comfort zones, increasing resilience, and creating opportunities, taking risks can help us achieve personal and professional growth and fulfillment. By approaching risks in a way that feels comfortable and safe for you, you can take the first steps towards overcoming your self-confidence blocks.

Surround yourself with positive people

The people we surround ourselves with can have a significant impact on our self-confidence. Negative and critical people can bring us down and reinforce our self-doubt, while positive and supportive people can help us feel more confident and capable. Surrounding ourselves with positive people is an important strategy for overcoming self-confidence blocks. In this section, we will discuss the benefits of surrounding ourselves with positive people and provide some tips for finding and building positive relationships.

Benefits of Surrounding Yourself with Positive People

1. Encouragement: Positive people provide encouragement and support, which can help us feel more confident in ourselves and our abilities.

2. Positive Feedback: Positive people tend to provide constructive and positive feedback, which can help us improve and grow.

3. Motivation: Positive people can motivate us to push ourselves and take on new challenges.

4. Inspiration: Positive people can inspire us with their own positive attitudes and actions, which can help us adopt more positive attitudes ourselves.

Tips for Finding and Building Positive Relationships

1. Identify Positive Role Models: Identify people in your life who exhibit positive traits and behaviors that you admire, and seek out opportunities to spend time with them.

2. Join Clubs or Groups: Joining clubs or groups that share your interests can help you meet new people who have similar values and interests.

3. Attend Events: Attend events such as conferences or workshops related to your interests or profession to meet like-minded individuals.

4. Volunteer: Volunteering for a cause you care about can connect you with people who share your values and passions.

5. Surround Yourself with Positive Media: Read books, listen to podcasts, and watch movies or shows that promote positivity and inspire you to be your best self.

6. Practice Active Listening: When you are spending time with positive people, make an effort to actively listen and engage with them. Ask questions, show interest, and be present in the moment.

7. Show Gratitude: Show gratitude towards the positive people in your life, and express your appreciation for their support and encouragement.

Conclusion

Surrounding ourselves with positive people is an essential strategy for overcoming self-confidence blocks. Positive people can provide us with encouragement, positive feedback, motivation, and inspiration. By identifying positive role models, joining clubs or groups, attending events, volunteering, surrounding ourselves with positive media, practicing active listening, and showing gratitude, we can build positive relationships and increase our self-confidence.

Practice positive self-talk

Positive self-talk is a powerful tool for overcoming self-doubt and building self-confidence. It involves replacing negative thoughts with positive, affirming ones. By doing this, you can change the way you feel about yourself and your abilities, which can help you overcome self-confidence blocks.

Here are some tips for practicing positive self-talk:

1. Recognize negative self-talk: The first step in practicing positive self-talk is to recognize when you are engaging in negative self-talk. Pay attention to the messages you are giving yourself and how they make you feel. If you find yourself thinking negative thoughts, challenge them and replace them with positive ones.

2. Be kind to yourself: When you make mistakes or face challenges, it's important to be kind to yourself. Instead of beating yourself up or being overly critical, practice self-compassion. Remind yourself that everyone makes mistakes and that you are doing the best you can.

3. Use positive affirmations: Positive affirmations are short, positive statements that you repeat to yourself. They can help you shift your mindset from negative to positive. Some examples of positive affirmations include "I am capable," "I am strong," and "I am worthy."

4. Use visualization: Visualization is a powerful technique for building self-confidence. When you visualize yourself succeeding, it can help you believe in your abilities and overcome self-doubt. Take some time each day to visualize yourself achieving your goals and feeling confident and self-assured.

5. Focus on your strengths: Instead of dwelling on your weaknesses or shortcomings, focus on your strengths. Identify your talents, skills, and accomplishments, and remind yourself of them regularly. This can help you feel more confident and capable.

6. Surround yourself with positive influences: Surrounding yourself with positive people and influences can help you feel more confident and optimistic. Seek out supportive friends and family members, join a positive social group, or listen to uplifting music or podcasts.

7. Practice gratitude: Gratitude is a powerful tool for shifting your focus from negativity to positivity. Take time each day to reflect on the things you are grateful for, such as your health, your relationships, and your accomplishments. This can help you cultivate a more positive mindset and build self-confidence.

By practicing positive self-talk, you can overcome self-confidence blocks and build a more positive, self-assured outlook on life. Remember, building self-confidence is a process, and it takes time and effort. But with practice and patience, you can achieve your goals and become the confident, self-assured person you want to be.

Chapter 4: Maintaining your self-confidence
Continue to challenge yourself

Once you have identified and worked to overcome your self-confidence blocks, it is important to continue to challenge yourself in order to maintain your newfound confidence. This means setting new goals and taking on new challenges to further develop your skills and abilities.

1. Set new goals: One of the best ways to continue to challenge yourself is by setting new goals. Think about what you want to achieve and create a plan to reach those goals. Make sure your goals are specific, measurable, achievable, relevant, and time-bound (SMART). By setting SMART goals, you can ensure that you have a clear idea of what you want to accomplish and how you plan to do it.

2. Embrace failure: Failure is a natural part of life, and it is essential to embrace it if you want to continue to challenge yourself. Failure provides an opportunity to learn and grow from your mistakes, and it can help you develop resilience and perseverance. When you encounter failure, try to reframe it as a learning experience rather than a setback.

3. Learn new skills: Continuing to learn new skills is a great way to challenge yourself and maintain your self-confidence. Learning new skills can help you build your knowledge base and increase your value in the workplace.

You can take classes, attend workshops or seminars, or simply read books on topics that interest you.

4. Step outside your comfort zone: It is important to continue to step outside your comfort zone if you want to maintain your self-confidence. This means taking on new challenges that may be uncomfortable or unfamiliar. When you step outside your comfort zone, you may experience fear or anxiety, but by pushing through these feelings, you can develop greater resilience and confidence.

5. Celebrate your successes: Celebrating your successes is essential for maintaining your self-confidence. When you achieve a goal or complete a challenging task, take time to acknowledge your accomplishments and reflect on your progress. Celebrating your successes can help you stay motivated and provide a sense of satisfaction and fulfillment.

6. Seek feedback: Seeking feedback from others can help you continue to grow and develop your skills. Feedback can help you identify areas where you need improvement and provide insight into your strengths and weaknesses. When seeking feedback, be open and receptive to constructive criticism, and use it as an opportunity to improve and grow.

7. Practice self-care: Taking care of yourself is essential for maintaining your self-confidence. This means

taking time to exercise, eat healthy foods, get enough sleep, and engage in activities that bring you joy and relaxation. When you prioritize self-care, you can improve your overall well-being and feel more confident and energized.

In conclusion, continuing to challenge yourself is an essential part of maintaining your self-confidence. By setting new goals, embracing failure, learning new skills, stepping outside your comfort zone, celebrating your successes, seeking feedback, and practicing self-care, you can continue to grow and develop your skills while maintaining your confidence and sense of self-worth.

Be patient

Building and maintaining self-confidence is a journey, not a destination. While you can make significant progress in overcoming self-doubt, it's important to remember that setbacks can and will happen. When they do, it's essential to be patient with yourself.

If you're used to being hard on yourself and have a habit of setting unrealistic expectations, learning to be patient can be challenging. However, it's critical to understand that self-confidence is not a linear progression. It's natural to have ups and downs along the way, and you're not alone in experiencing setbacks.

Here are some strategies for cultivating patience as you work to maintain your self-confidence:

1. Set realistic expectations

When it comes to building and maintaining self-confidence, it's essential to set realistic expectations for yourself. Understand that progress takes time and that setbacks are a normal part of the process. Don't expect to be completely confident overnight or to never experience doubt again. Be kind to yourself and give yourself permission to make mistakes.

2. Celebrate small wins

As you work to maintain your self-confidence, celebrate the small wins along the way. Recognize when you've pushed yourself out of your comfort zone, even if it's a small step. Celebrating these accomplishments can help keep you motivated and remind you of the progress you're making.

3. Practice self-compassion

Self-compassion involves treating yourself with the same kindness, concern, and support that you would offer to a close friend. When you experience setbacks or challenges, be gentle with yourself. Recognize that it's okay to make mistakes and that setbacks are an opportunity for growth and learning.

4. Learn from setbacks

Instead of beating yourself up over setbacks, use them as an opportunity to learn and grow. Reflect on what went wrong and what you can do differently next time. Remember that setbacks are not failures, and they don't define you or your abilities.

5. Stay committed to your goals

Maintaining self-confidence requires ongoing effort and commitment. Stay focused on your goals and keep working towards them, even when progress feels slow or you experience setbacks. Remember why you started on this journey and what you hope to achieve. Keeping your goals in mind can help you stay motivated and focused on the bigger picture.

6. Seek support

Finally, don't be afraid to seek support from others. Whether it's talking to a friend, family member, or therapist, having someone to lean on can make a significant difference in maintaining your self-confidence. Surround yourself with people who uplift and support you, and who can remind you of your strengths and accomplishments when you need it most.

Conclusion:

Maintaining self-confidence requires ongoing effort and patience. While setbacks and challenges are a normal part of the process, by setting realistic expectations, celebrating small wins, practicing self-compassion, learning from setbacks, staying committed to your goals, and seeking support, you can continue to build and maintain your self-confidence over time. Remember that self-confidence is a journey, not a destination, and be patient with yourself along the way.

Celebrate your successes

When it comes to maintaining your self-confidence, celebrating your successes is an important aspect to consider. Celebrating your successes means taking the time to recognize and acknowledge your achievements, big or small. It can help boost your confidence and motivation, and remind you that you are capable of achieving your goals.

Here are some tips on how to celebrate your successes:

1. Reflect on your achievements: Take a few moments to reflect on what you have accomplished. Write down your successes and the steps you took to achieve them. This will help you remember your accomplishments and boost your confidence.

2. Share your successes: Share your achievements with someone who supports and encourages you. This could be a friend, family member, or mentor. Sharing your successes can help you feel proud and give you a sense of validation.

3. Treat yourself: Treat yourself to something special to celebrate your success. This could be something as simple as a favorite snack, a night out with friends, or buying yourself something you've been wanting for a while. Treating

yourself can help you feel good about your achievements and motivate you to keep going.

4. Take time to appreciate: Take time to appreciate your success and the effort you put in to achieve it. This could mean taking a moment to savor your accomplishment or taking a break to relax and recharge.

5. Set new goals: Celebrating your successes can help you feel motivated and confident to set new goals for yourself. Use your success as a reminder that you are capable of achieving your goals and don't be afraid to set new, challenging ones.

Remember, celebrating your successes is an important part of maintaining your self-confidence. It can help you stay motivated, appreciate your accomplishments, and continue to strive for new goals.

Chapter 5: Dealing with setbacks
Don't give up

Dealing with setbacks is an inevitable part of life, and it can be especially challenging when you're trying to build and maintain self-confidence. When you face setbacks, it's easy to become discouraged and start to doubt yourself. However, it's important to remember that setbacks are not failures, but rather opportunities to learn and grow. In this chapter, we'll explore strategies for overcoming setbacks and staying on track in your self-confidence journey.

One of the most important things to remember when dealing with setbacks is to not give up. It's easy to feel defeated when you encounter obstacles or face rejection, but it's important to maintain a positive attitude and keep moving forward. Here are some strategies for staying motivated and not giving up in the face of setbacks:

1. Reframe your mindset: When you encounter setbacks, it's easy to fall into a negative mindset and start to doubt yourself. Instead, try to reframe your mindset and focus on the opportunities for growth and learning that come with setbacks. Ask yourself what you can learn from the experience, and how you can use that knowledge to improve and move forward.

2. Stay focused on your goals: Setbacks can be distracting and cause you to lose sight of your goals. To stay on track, it's important to stay focused on your goals and remind yourself of why they are important to you. Visualize yourself achieving your goals and use that vision to stay motivated and focused.

3. Practice self-compassion: It's easy to be hard on yourself when you encounter setbacks, but it's important to practice self-compassion and be kind to yourself. Remember that setbacks are a natural part of the journey, and be gentle with yourself as you work through them.

4. Reach out for support: When you're feeling discouraged or overwhelmed, it's important to reach out for support. Talk to a trusted friend, family member, or mentor who can offer encouragement and help you stay motivated.

5. Keep taking action: Even when you're facing setbacks, it's important to keep taking action towards your goals. Break your goals down into smaller, more manageable steps and focus on making progress, even if it's just a little bit each day.

6. Use setbacks as motivation: Instead of letting setbacks defeat you, use them as motivation to work harder and be even more determined to succeed. When you

encounter obstacles, use them as fuel to keep pushing yourself towards your goals.

7. Keep a positive attitude: Maintaining a positive attitude can be challenging when you're facing setbacks, but it's essential for staying motivated and not giving up. Focus on the positives, even if they seem small, and try to stay optimistic about the future.

In conclusion, setbacks are a natural part of the self-confidence journey, and it's important to be prepared to face them. By using these strategies and staying focused on your goals, you can overcome setbacks and continue to build and maintain self-confidence. Remember, setbacks are not failures, but rather opportunities to learn and grow. Don't give up, and keep pushing yourself towards your goals.

Learn from your mistakes

Self-confidence is not a linear process, and setbacks are a common experience. It's important to understand that making mistakes and experiencing failures are normal parts of life. However, it's how we respond to these setbacks that can either lead to growth or hold us back. In this section, we will explore how to learn from mistakes and setbacks to ultimately strengthen our self-confidence.

Acknowledge Your Mistakes

The first step in learning from mistakes is to acknowledge them. It can be tempting to ignore or minimize our mistakes, but this approach only prevents us from growing and improving. By acknowledging our mistakes, we can confront them head-on and begin to develop a plan for improvement.

Take Responsibility

Once you've acknowledged your mistake, it's important to take responsibility for it. This means owning up to your role in the situation and not blaming others. Taking responsibility for your mistakes shows maturity and integrity and can help you move forward with a clear conscience.

Analyze the Mistake

After acknowledging your mistake and taking responsibility for it, the next step is to analyze the situation.

Look at what went wrong and identify what factors contributed to the mistake. This step can help you understand what went wrong and prevent similar mistakes from happening in the future.

Identify What You Can Control

When analyzing the mistake, it's essential to identify what you can control. Often, there are external factors that contribute to our mistakes that are beyond our control. However, it's important to focus on what you can control, such as your actions and reactions. By identifying what you can control, you can develop a plan to prevent similar mistakes in the future.

Develop a Plan for Improvement

After analyzing the mistake and identifying what you can control, the next step is to develop a plan for improvement. This plan should focus on specific actions you can take to prevent similar mistakes in the future. Be sure to set measurable goals and track your progress.

Practice Self-Compassion

Learning from mistakes can be a challenging and emotionally charged process. It's essential to practice self-compassion throughout this process. Remember that making mistakes is a natural part of growth, and be kind to yourself throughout the process. Negative self-talk and self-criticism only hold you back and prevent growth.

Seek Support

Finally, don't be afraid to seek support during this process. Talking to a trusted friend or mentor can help you gain perspective and develop a plan for improvement. Additionally, seeking the help of a therapist or counselor can help you process your emotions and develop coping strategies.

Conclusion

Learning from mistakes is an essential part of building self-confidence. By acknowledging our mistakes, taking responsibility, analyzing the situation, identifying what we can control, developing a plan for improvement, practicing self-compassion, and seeking support, we can grow and ultimately strengthen our self-confidence. Remember that setbacks are a natural part of the process, and learning from them is key to long-term growth and success.

Don't compare yourself to others

Introduction: Comparing yourself to others is a common habit that can negatively impact your self-confidence and self-esteem. It's natural to want to evaluate your own abilities and achievements against those of others, but when taken to an extreme, it can lead to feelings of inadequacy and self-doubt. In this section, we'll explore the dangers of comparing yourself to others and offer some strategies for breaking this harmful habit.

The Dangers of Comparison: Comparing yourself to others can be dangerous for several reasons. Firstly, it's important to recognize that everyone has their unique strengths, weaknesses, and life experiences. Comparing yourself to someone who has different abilities or life circumstances is not an accurate or fair comparison. This can lead to feelings of inadequacy, even if you are successful in your own right.

Secondly, comparisons can be misleading. Social media, in particular, has made it easier than ever to compare yourself to others' carefully curated highlight reels. People typically only share their best moments online, which can make it seem like everyone else has it all together while you're struggling. This is simply not true, and comparing yourself to others online is a recipe for feeling inferior.

Finally, comparisons can be demotivating. If you're constantly comparing yourself to someone else who is more successful, you may feel discouraged and unmotivated to pursue your own goals. This can lead to a vicious cycle of self-doubt and self-sabotage, which can ultimately prevent you from achieving your full potential.

Strategies for Breaking the Habit: Breaking the habit of comparing yourself to others is not easy, but it is possible. Here are some strategies that can help:

1. Focus on your own progress: Instead of comparing yourself to others, focus on your own progress. Set goals for yourself and work towards achieving them, regardless of what others are doing. Celebrate your own successes and milestones, no matter how small they may seem.

2. Practice gratitude: Practicing gratitude can help you appreciate what you have and shift your focus away from what you don't have. Take time each day to reflect on what you're grateful for in your life, whether it's your health, your job, or your relationships.

3. Recognize your strengths: Instead of focusing on your weaknesses or areas for improvement, take time to recognize your strengths. What are you good at? What do others appreciate about you? When you focus on your strengths, you build self-confidence and self-esteem.

4. Limit social media: Social media can be a breeding ground for comparison. If you find yourself constantly comparing yourself to others online, consider limiting your social media use or taking a break altogether.

5. Be kind to yourself: Remember that nobody is perfect, and everyone has their own struggles and insecurities. Be kind to yourself and practice self-compassion. Treat yourself the way you would treat a friend who was going through a tough time.

Conclusion: Comparing yourself to others can be a harmful habit that can negatively impact your self-confidence and self-esteem. By recognizing the dangers of comparison and implementing strategies for breaking the habit, you can build a stronger sense of self-confidence and self-worth. Remember to focus on your own progress, practice gratitude, recognize your strengths, limit social media, and be kind to yourself. With time and effort, you can break the cycle of comparison and achieve your full potential.

Celebrate your successes

Self-confidence is not just about overcoming obstacles and dealing with setbacks. It's also about acknowledging and celebrating your successes, no matter how big or small they may be. Celebrating your successes can help you build and maintain your self-confidence, as well as keep you motivated and inspired to achieve more.

In this section, we'll explore the importance of celebrating your successes and provide some tips on how to do it effectively.

Why Celebrating Your Successes is Important

When you celebrate your successes, you're essentially giving yourself a pat on the back for a job well done. This positive reinforcement can help to boost your self-confidence and motivate you to continue pursuing your goals.

Here are some specific benefits of celebrating your successes:

1. It helps you stay motivated: Celebrating your successes can help you stay motivated and inspired to keep working towards your goals. When you acknowledge your progress, you're more likely to stay on track and keep pushing forward.

2. It builds your self-confidence: Celebrating your successes can help to build your self-confidence by

reminding you of your capabilities and accomplishments. When you recognize what you've achieved, you'll feel more confident in your abilities to take on future challenges.

3. It creates positive emotions: Celebrating your successes can create positive emotions like joy, happiness, and excitement. These positive emotions can help to counteract any negative feelings you may have about setbacks or failures, and keep you focused on the positive aspects of your journey.

4. It helps to reduce stress: Celebrating your successes can help to reduce stress by giving you a sense of accomplishment and validation. When you're feeling stressed or overwhelmed, taking a moment to celebrate what you've achieved can help to ease your anxiety and calm your mind.

Tips for Celebrating Your Successes

Now that we've discussed why celebrating your successes is important, let's explore some tips on how to do it effectively:

1. Set specific milestones: To make it easier to celebrate your successes, try setting specific milestones along the way. This could be as simple as breaking down a larger goal into smaller, achievable steps, and celebrating each one as you complete it.

2. Choose your own rewards: When you celebrate your successes, choose rewards that are meaningful to you. This could be anything from treating yourself to a favorite meal or activity, to taking a day off to relax and recharge.

3. Share your successes with others: Celebrating your successes with others can help to make the experience more meaningful and enjoyable. Consider sharing your achievements with friends, family, or colleagues who will be supportive and happy for you.

4. Keep a record of your successes: Keeping a record of your successes can help you to stay motivated and remind you of your progress. This could be as simple as jotting down your accomplishments in a journal or planner, or creating a vision board to visualize your goals and achievements.

5. Practice gratitude: Practicing gratitude can help to enhance the positive emotions you feel when celebrating your successes. Take a moment to reflect on the people, circumstances, and opportunities that have contributed to your achievements, and express gratitude for them.

Conclusion

Celebrating your successes is an important part of building and maintaining your self-confidence. By acknowledging your progress and achievements, you can stay motivated, build your self-confidence, and create positive emotions that will help you to overcome setbacks and challenges.

Remember to set specific milestones, choose your own rewards, share your successes with others, keep a record of your successes, and practice gratitude. These tips can help you to celebrate your successes effectively and enjoyably, and keep you inspired and motivated to achieve even more in the future.

Chapter 6: Finding your inner confidence
What is inner confidence?

Inner confidence, also known as self-assurance, is the ability to trust in oneself and one's abilities. It is a deep sense of self-belief that comes from within and enables individuals to face challenges and navigate life with a sense of ease and self-assurance. Inner confidence is not dependent on external validation or approval, but is rooted in an individual's internal beliefs and attitudes.

Unlike external confidence, which may be based on one's appearance, social status, or other external factors, inner confidence is not tied to any particular external trait or accomplishment. Instead, it is a reflection of an individual's overall sense of self-worth and their ability to trust in themselves and their abilities.

Inner confidence is not something that can be acquired overnight, nor is it something that can be given to someone by another person. It is a process that involves self-reflection, self-awareness, and self-improvement. It requires a willingness to be vulnerable, to confront one's fears and weaknesses, and to take risks in order to grow and develop.

So, how can one develop inner confidence? Here are some tips:

1. Develop a growth mindset: A growth mindset is the belief that one's abilities can be developed through dedication and hard work. It is the opposite of a fixed mindset, which is the belief that one's abilities are fixed and cannot be changed. By adopting a growth mindset, individuals can cultivate a sense of optimism and self-assurance that comes from knowing that they can improve and develop their abilities.

2. Practice self-compassion: Self-compassion is the practice of treating oneself with kindness and understanding, especially in times of difficulty or failure. By practicing self-compassion, individuals can develop a greater sense of self-acceptance and self-love, which are key components of inner confidence.

3. Embrace vulnerability: Vulnerability is the willingness to expose oneself to the possibility of harm or rejection. It is often seen as a weakness, but in reality, it is a strength. By embracing vulnerability, individuals can develop a deeper sense of authenticity and self-awareness, which are important components of inner confidence.

4. Develop a strong sense of purpose: Having a strong sense of purpose can help individuals to feel more confident and self-assured. When one has a clear sense of what they

want to achieve and why it is important to them, they are more likely to feel motivated and focused.

5. Cultivate positive relationships: Positive relationships can provide a sense of support and validation that can help to boost one's confidence. By surrounding oneself with people who are supportive, caring, and positive, individuals can develop a greater sense of self-worth and confidence.

In summary, inner confidence is a deep sense of self-belief that comes from within. It is not dependent on external factors and requires self-reflection, self-awareness, and self-improvement to develop. By cultivating a growth mindset, practicing self-compassion, embracing vulnerability, developing a strong sense of purpose, and cultivating positive relationships, individuals can develop a strong sense of inner confidence that will serve them well throughout their lives.

How to find your inner confidence

If you're struggling with self-confidence, you may feel like you'll never be able to find your inner confidence. But the truth is that everyone has the potential to be confident, it just takes some work. Here are some tips for finding your inner confidence:

1. Start with self-acceptance

The first step to finding your inner confidence is to accept yourself for who you are. It's important to acknowledge your flaws and imperfections, but don't let them define you. Recognize your strengths and focus on what you like about yourself. Remember that everyone has flaws, and they don't make you any less worthy of confidence.

2. Practice self-care

Taking care of yourself is a crucial part of building inner confidence. Make sure to get enough sleep, eat healthy foods, and exercise regularly. Take time for yourself to do things that make you feel good, whether it's taking a bath, reading a book, or spending time with friends. When you feel good physically, it's easier to feel good mentally.

3. Identify your values

Knowing your values can help you make decisions and feel more confident in yourself. Take some time to think about what's important to you in life. This could be things like honesty, kindness, creativity, or family. Once you've identified your values, make an effort to live your life in a way that aligns with them.

4. Set achievable goals

Setting goals and working towards them can help build confidence in your abilities. Start with small goals that you know you can achieve, and gradually work your way up to bigger goals. When you accomplish something, take time to celebrate your success and acknowledge the hard work you put in.

5. Practice positive self-talk

The way you talk to yourself can have a big impact on your confidence. Try to replace negative self-talk with positive affirmations. Instead of saying "I'm not good enough," try saying "I'm doing my best," or "I have what it takes to succeed." When you believe in yourself, it's easier to feel confident.

6. Surround yourself with positive people

The people you spend time with can have a big impact on your confidence. Surround yourself with people who support and encourage you, and who make you feel good about yourself. Avoid people who bring you down or make you feel insecure.

7. Embrace your uniqueness

No one else in the world is exactly like you, and that's something to be celebrated. Embrace your uniqueness and don't try to be someone you're not. When you accept and love yourself for who you are, you'll naturally feel more confident.

8. Take risks

Stepping outside of your comfort zone can be scary, but it can also be incredibly empowering. Take small risks and try new things. When you succeed, you'll feel more confident in your abilities. And even if you fail, you'll learn from the experience and grow as a person.

9. Practice mindfulness

Mindfulness can help you stay grounded and present in the moment. When you're mindful, you're less likely to get caught up in negative thoughts and self-doubt. Try practicing mindfulness through activities like meditation, yoga, or simply taking a few deep breaths throughout the day.

10. Seek support

Sometimes finding your inner confidence can be a difficult journey, and it's okay to seek support along the way. Consider talking to a therapist or counselor who can help you work through your feelings of self-doubt and build your confidence. Remember that there's no shame in asking for help, and that seeking support is a sign of strength.

Finding your inner confidence takes time and effort, but it's worth it. When you feel confident in yourself, you can take on challenges and achieve your goals with ease. Remember that inner confidence is not just about how you appear on the outside, but it also comes from within. Here are some tips on how to find your inner confidence:

1. Identify your strengths and weaknesses: Knowing your strengths will help you focus on what you are good at, while identifying your weaknesses will help you work on them.

2. Practice self-care: Taking care of your physical and mental health is crucial in building inner confidence. This includes getting enough sleep, eating a healthy diet, exercising regularly, and practicing self-compassion.

3. Set realistic goals: Setting achievable goals that align with your strengths can help boost your confidence as you work towards them.

4. Embrace failure: Instead of viewing failure as a setback, try to see it as an opportunity to learn and grow. This mindset can help build resilience and inner confidence.

5. Surround yourself with positive influences: Spend time with people who uplift and support you, and distance yourself from negative influences that can bring you down.

6. Challenge yourself: Stepping out of your comfort zone and taking on new challenges can help you build confidence in your abilities and push you towards achieving your goals.

Remember that building inner confidence is a process that takes time and effort, but the rewards are worth it. By practicing self-care, setting realistic goals, embracing failure, surrounding yourself with positive influences, and challenging yourself, you can find your inner confidence and achieve your dreams.

Conclusion
The importance of inner confidence

The concept of inner confidence is an essential component of a fulfilling and successful life. It's not just about having the right skills or knowledge, but also about believing in yourself and your abilities. Inner confidence allows you to take on challenges, navigate difficult situations, and achieve your goals with greater ease and resilience.

Inner confidence goes beyond external validation, such as the approval of others or material possessions. It comes from within and is cultivated through a combination of self-awareness, self-acceptance, and self-improvement. When you have inner confidence, you are less likely to be affected by external circumstances and more likely to persevere through obstacles and setbacks.

One of the most significant benefits of inner confidence is its impact on mental health and well-being. Low self-esteem and lack of confidence can lead to anxiety, depression, and other mental health issues. In contrast, inner confidence promotes a positive mindset, emotional resilience, and greater satisfaction with life.

Additionally, inner confidence can positively impact various areas of life, including career success, relationships, and personal growth. In the workplace, confident individuals are more likely to be promoted, take on leadership roles, and succeed in challenging projects. In relationships, confidence can lead to better communication, more meaningful connections, and greater satisfaction. In personal growth, inner confidence can inspire you to take on new challenges, pursue your passions, and live a more fulfilling life.

It's important to note that inner confidence is not a fixed trait but a skill that can be developed and strengthened over time. With practice, you can learn to overcome self-doubt and negative self-talk, identify and challenge limiting beliefs, and cultivate a more positive and resilient mindset.

In conclusion, inner confidence is a crucial ingredient for a fulfilling and successful life. It allows you to face challenges with greater ease, improves mental health and well-being, and positively impacts various areas of life. Developing inner confidence requires time and effort, but the rewards are immeasurable. With a commitment to self-awareness, self-acceptance, and self-improvement, anyone can find and cultivate their inner confidence.

How to continue to build your inner confidence

Building inner confidence is an ongoing process that requires continuous effort and dedication. It's important to remember that confidence is not a fixed state but rather a mindset that can be cultivated and strengthened over time. Here are some tips on how to continue to build your inner confidence:

1. Practice self-care: Taking care of your physical and mental health is essential to building inner confidence. Make sure you are getting enough sleep, eating a healthy diet, and exercising regularly. Additionally, make time for activities that bring you joy and relaxation, such as meditation or spending time in nature.

2. Surround yourself with positivity: Surround yourself with people who uplift and encourage you. Stay away from negative influences and toxic relationships that can bring you down. Instead, seek out people who inspire you and challenge you to be your best self.

3. Embrace failure: Failure is a natural part of life, and it's important to embrace it as a learning opportunity rather than a setback. When you experience failure, take time to reflect on what went wrong and what you can do differently next time. Remember, every failure brings you one step closer to success.

4. Focus on your strengths: Instead of dwelling on your weaknesses, focus on your strengths and the things you are good at. By recognizing and developing your talents, you can build a strong sense of self-esteem and confidence in your abilities.

5. Take risks: Stepping out of your comfort zone and taking risks can help you build confidence and resilience. When you take on new challenges, you develop new skills and gain valuable experience, which can boost your self-confidence.

6. Set realistic goals: Setting achievable goals and working towards them can help you build confidence in your abilities. Start small and gradually work your way up to bigger goals. Celebrate your successes along the way, no matter how small they may seem.

7. Practice positive self-talk: The way you talk to yourself can have a big impact on your confidence levels. Instead of criticizing yourself, practice positive self-talk by using affirmations and focusing on your strengths and achievements.

8. Continue to learn and grow: Learning new things and developing new skills can help you build confidence in your abilities. Take courses, attend workshops, and seek out

mentors who can help you grow both personally and professionally.

In conclusion, building inner confidence is a journey that requires patience, perseverance, and self-reflection. By practicing self-care, surrounding yourself with positivity, embracing failure, focusing on your strengths, taking risks, setting realistic goals, practicing positive self-talk, and continuing to learn and grow, you can build the inner confidence you need to achieve your goals and live a fulfilling life. Remember, building inner confidence is not a destination but a lifelong process, and the more you invest in yourself, the more confident and resilient you will become.

THE END

Wordbook

Welcome to the glossary section of this book. Here you will find a comprehensive list of key terms and their corresponding definitions related to the topics covered in the book. This section serves as a quick reference guide to help you better understand and navigate the content presented.

1. Self-confidence: The belief in one's abilities, qualities, and judgment.

2. Self-esteem: A person's overall sense of self-worth or value.

3. Self-efficacy: The belief in one's ability to accomplish specific tasks or goals.

4. Self-talk: The internal dialogue or thoughts a person has about themselves.

5. Inner critic: The voice or thoughts in a person's mind that is critical or negative towards themselves.

6. Self-compassion: The practice of treating oneself with kindness and understanding during times of difficulty or failure.

7. Resilience: The ability to recover from setbacks or difficulties and bounce back stronger.

8. Positive psychology: A field of psychology that focuses on the positive aspects of human experience, such as happiness, well-being, and flourishing.

9. Growth mindset: The belief that abilities and intelligence can be developed and improved through hard work and dedication.

10. Fixed mindset: The belief that abilities and intelligence are set and cannot be changed.

Supplementary Materials

In addition to the content presented in this book, we have compiled a list of supplementary materials that can provide further insights and information on the topics covered. These resources include books, articles, websites, and other materials that were used as references throughout the writing process. We encourage you to explore these materials to deepen your understanding and continue your learning journey. Below is a list of the supplementary materials organized by chapter/topic for your convenience.

Introduction:

No specific references are needed for the introduction section.

Chapter 1: The different types of self-confidence blocks

Branden, N. (1994). The six pillars of self-esteem. Bantam.

Cherry, K. (2021). What is self-esteem? Verywell Mind. Retrieved from https://www.verywellmind.com/what-is-self-esteem-2795868

Chapter 2: How to identify your self-confidence blocks

Burns, D. D. (1980). Feeling good: The new mood therapy. New American Library.

Cherry, K. (2021). What is self-esteem? Verywell Mind. Retrieved from https://www.verywellmind.com/what-is-self-esteem-2795868

Chapter 3: Overcoming your self-confidence blocks

Bandura, A. (1997). Self-efficacy: The exercise of control. W.H. Freeman and Company.

Brown, B. (2010). The gifts of imperfection: Let go of who you think you're supposed to be and embrace who you are. Hazelden.

Chapter 4: Maintaining your self-confidence

Adams, J. S. (1965). Inequity in social exchange. Advances in Experimental Social Psychology, 2, 267-299.

Seligman, M. E. (2011). Flourish: A visionary new understanding of happiness and well-being. Simon and Schuster.

Chapter 5: Dealing with setbacks

Dweck, C. S. (2006). Mindset: The new psychology of success. Ballantine Books.

Fredrickson, B. L. (2001). The role of positive emotions in positive psychology: The broaden-and-build theory of positive emotions. American Psychologist, 56(3), 218-226.

Chapter 6: Finding your inner confidence

Cherry, K. (2021). What is self-esteem? Verywell Mind. Retrieved from https://www.verywellmind.com/what-is-self-esteem-2795868

McGonigal, K. (2013). The willpower instinct: How self-control works, why it matters, and what you can do to get more of it. Avery.

Conclusion

No specific references are needed for the conclusion section.

www.ingramcontent.com/pod-product-compliance
Lightning Source LLC
LaVergne TN
LVHW012126070526
838202LV00056B/5871